This book belongs to:

Sera and Ethan

It was given to me by:

Grandmother

On:

2/3/12

Bible
Animal Stories
for Bedtime

JANE LANDRETH
ILLUSTRATED BY DAVID MILES

BARBOUR
PUBLISHING

© 2011 by Barbour Publishing, Inc.

ISBN 978-1-61626-339-3

Cover and interior illustration: David Miles Illustration, www.davidmiles.com

Published by Barbour Publishing, Inc., P.O. Box 719, Uhrichsville, Ohio 44683 www.barbourbooks.com

Our mission is to publish and distribute inspirational products offering exceptional value and biblical encouragement to the masses.

Member of the
Evangelical Christian
Publishers Association

Printed in China.
Leo Paper, Gulao Town, Heshan City, Guangdong, China; September 2011; D10002886

To my grandsons, Lane and Cody,
who enjoy Grandma reading
stories to them.

"Ask the animals, and they
will teach you, or the birds in the sky,
and they will tell you. . .
or let the fish in the sea inform you."

Job 12:7-8 NIV

Contents

God Created the Animals

So God made the wild animals, the
tame animals, and all the small crawling
animals to produce more of their own
kind. God saw that this was good.

Genesis 1:25 NCV

Our wonderful God made all kinds of creatures, each one of a different shape, color, size, and attitude! God created the animals to live in the water and in the air first. Next He created the animals to live on the land. Then He made Adam, the first man, to take care of them all. And it only took God two days to make all those things. Wow! What an awesome Creator!

God made the giant forty-foot-tall dinosaurs and the tiny insect that was only the size of a pinhead. He gave animals eight legs, six legs, four legs, or two legs, and some no legs at all. Some animals had arms and some did not. Some animals had long necks and some short necks. Some had no necks. Some animals had fur, some had scales, some had feathers, and some had smooth skin. God made animals fat, skinny, tall, and short.

God made animals to live on the ground and some to live in trees. He made some animals to live on the tall mountains, some to live under the ground, some to fly in the sky, and some to swim in the deepest oceans. God created humans, too, each one different from the other. And it was all good. Wow! What a great God!

Dear God, thank You for
making so many different kinds
of creatures, including me!
It's wonderful that we are
not all the same. Amen.

The First Lamb Sacrifice

Abel brought the best parts from some of the firstborn of his flock. The Lord accepted Abel and his gift, but he did not accept Cain and his gift.

Genesis 4:4–5 NCV

God likes good gifts, just like we do! This is a story about the first gifts given to God. One of these gifts was a lamb, which is a baby sheep. Each baby lamb makes its own high-sounding noise called bleating. This is the way the mother sheep can know her own baby lamb.

In the Bible, the first human mother, Eve, and the first human father, Adam, had a baby boy. They named him Cain. Then they had a second boy and named him Abel. Cain worked the land and raised food. Abel took care of sheep and raised lambs.

One day Cain brought some of his garden vegetables to God. This was not the offering God wanted Cain to bring. So God was not pleased with Cain and his gift. And Cain became very angry.

God said to Cain, "Why are you angry? Do what is right and bring the right kind of gift. Then I will accept your gift."

Abel brought some of the fattest parts of his best lambs as gifts for God. They were the male lambs that were born first. God was pleased with Abel and his gifts.

We don't sacrifice animals anymore. But God does want us to bring our best to Him by praying and by doing the right thing.

Dear God, You like good gifts—
just like me! I want to bring
You the best that I have.
Help me to always do what
pleases You. Amen.

The Animals on the Ark

The clean animals, the unclean animals, the birds, and everything that crawls on the ground came to Noah. They went into the boat in groups of two, male and female, just as God had commanded Noah.

Genesis 7:8–9 NCV

There are millions and millions of different creatures living in the world today. Now imagine how big Noah's ark had to be to hold two of every animal in the world. It had to be gigantic!

Zzzz-zzz went the saws. Bang, bang, bang went the hammers. God told Noah to build a big boat. The people laughed at Noah when they saw such a big boat sitting on dry land. But Noah and his sons just kept on sawing and hammering.

Soon the boat was finished. God told Noah to take two of every animal into the ark. Two lions padded into the boat. Two rabbits hopped in. Two ducks waddled in. Two kangaroos jumped into the ark. Two snakes crawled in. Two hippopotamuses thumped in. Two birds flew in. Two of every kind of animal, bird, and crawling creature went into the boat.

Then Noah and his family went into the boat. And God shut the door!

It began to rain. It rained and rained and rained. The water got deeper and deeper. The big boat floated on the water. Noah believed in God's promises, and God didn't let him sink! He kept Noah's family and all the animals safe.

Dear God, like Noah, I believe in Your promises. I know You will never let me down. So no matter what, I can be brave, just like Noah. Amen.

The Raven and the Dove

He [Noah] sent a raven out. It kept
flying back and forth until the
water had dried up from the earth.
Then Noah sent a dove out.

Genesis 8:7–8 NIRV

Ravens and doves are awesome birds. A raven has powerful wings, will eat almost anything, and can fly for a long time without resting. It makes its nest in high places. The dove also has powerful wings but stays closer to the ground and eats mostly plants. Noah used these two birds to help him find out if the floodwaters had gone down.

Noah and his family had been in the ark for many, many days. When the rain stopped, God sent a wind to blow. The water began to go down.

When the ark stopped floating, Noah opened the window and sent out a raven. The bird had mighty wings, so it flew back and forth until it found a place to rest.

Noah waited a while longer then sent out a dove. The dove came back because it could not find any place to rest. Later Noah sent out the dove again. By evening, it came back with a leaf in its bill. Noah knew the earth would soon be dry and his family and all the animals could leave the ark.

When God created birds, He knew the raven and the dove would need powerful wings for a special job. When God created you, He gave you gifts for a special job, too. Wonder what that will be.

Thank You, God, for creating animals and people with special gifts that we can use to serve You and each other. Amen.

An Animal Offering to God

The LORD said to Abram, "Bring me a three-year-old cow, a three-year-old goat, a three-year-old male sheep, a dove and a young pigeon."

Genesis 15:9 NCV

In the Old Testament, God asked people to sacrifice animals. Sometimes those sacrifices were made to worship God. Sometimes they stood for a promise from God to a man.

God made a promise to Abram one day. He came to Abram in a vision and told him that he would be blessed. Then God took Abram outside and said, "Look up at the sky. Count the stars, if you can. You will have that many children."

Abram believed God. God asked Abram to bring some animals to Him—a three-year-old cow, a three-year-old goat, a three-year-old male sheep, a dove, and a young pigeon—for a sacrifice.

Abram brought the animals to God

and cut them into two pieces. As the sun was going down in the sky, Abram fell into a deep sleep. Soon it was dark all around. A burning torch and a firepot filled with smoke appeared. They passed between the pieces of the animals.

God made a promise to Abram on that day. He would bless Abram's children and their children and all the children who came later.

God promises to bless you and all His other children today—but an animal sacrifice is not needed.

God, I'm glad I am Your child.
Thank You for blessing me.
Amen.

A Calf Fed Abraham's Guests

Then he [Abraham] brought
some butter and milk and the
calf that had been prepared.
He served them to the three men.

Genesis 18:8 NIrV

A baby cow is called a *calf*. In Bible times, a calf was important because it was used to provide special meals for special people.

One day Abraham was sitting outside his tent in the shade. He looked up and saw three men standing nearby. He quickly left his tent to meet them. Abraham bowed low to the ground because he recognized two of them as angels and the third one as the Lord.

"Let me get a little water to wash your feet," said Abraham. "You can rest under the tree. I will get you something to eat, too."

While the three men rested, Abraham hurried into the tent and said to Sarah, his wife, "Quick! Get some flour and bake some bread."

Then Abraham ran to the herd of cattle. He picked out a special calf and gave it to the servant. The servant hurried to prepare the calf.

Soon Abraham brought butter, milk, and the cooked calf to the three men. He served them and visited with them.

Even though Abraham was a rich, powerful man, he hurried to serve his guests. He washed their feet. Then he pleased them with a good meal of veal and bread and milk. This, in turn, pleased God. Are you willing to serve the guests that visit your home?

Dear God, help me to be kind
to people who visit my house
and to offer them the best
food that we have. Amen.

A Ram Is Provided

Abraham looked up and there in a
thicket he saw a ram caught by its
horns. He went over and took the
ram and sacrificed it as a burnt
offering instead of his son.

Genesis 22:13 NIV

A male sheep is called a *ram*. Rams have horns to fight off wild animals and other male sheep. In the Bible, rams were used as a sacrifice offering. One day God asked Abraham to make a sacrifice offering.

God spoke to Abraham. "Take your son, Isaac, to a place I will show you. Give your son as an offering to Me."

Abraham loved God, but giving up his only son, Isaac, was a very hard thing to do. Abraham loved Isaac but he did not argue with God. He took Isaac with him to the mountain God showed him.

On the climb up the mountain, Isaac asked, "Father, we have the wood and fire, but where is the offering?"

Abraham answered, "God will give us one."

Isaac helped Abraham build an altar. Then Abraham laid his son on the altar as an offering, just as God had asked. Suddenly God's angel spoke. "Abraham! Do not hurt your son." Abraham looked up and saw a ram. Its horns had gotten caught in a bush. Instead of sacrificing his son, Abraham sacrificed the ram God had provided.

God provided the ram for Isaac. Later God provided Jesus for the whole world. When our hearts obey and trust in God, He always delivers—no matter what!

Dear God, sometimes I'm asked
to do something hard—even
something I don't want to do.
Give me courage to obey You
because You always know
what is best. Amen.

Camels at Rebekah's Well

After he finished drinking,
Rebekah said, "I will also pour
some water for your camels."
Genesis 24:19 NCV

A camel is a good animal for traveling through the hot, dry desert. The camel can go without water for a long time. It can carry a heavy load on its hump just like it did for Abraham's servant.

Abraham called his servant to him. "Go into a far country to find a wife for my son, Isaac," he said. "God will go ahead of you and show you what to do."

So the servant loaded camels with gifts and traveled to a far country. He stopped near a well outside town and made the thirsty camels kneel down. Then he waited for the women to come to the well for water.

"God, show me the young woman to whom I will speak," prayed the servant.

"If she gives me a drink and waters my camels, I will know that is the one You have chosen for Isaac."

Before long, Rebekah came to the well for water. She gave the servant a drink and then said, "I will also give your camels a drink."

The servant knew Rebekah was the wife God had picked for Isaac.

God uses many things of this world to guide us. Here He used camels and a praying servant. Lift your prayers to God, then look for His guidance.

Dear God, I know that You will
always answer my prayers.
Thank You for showing me what
to do when I ask. Help me to
follow Your answer. Amen.

Jacob's Animal Gifts

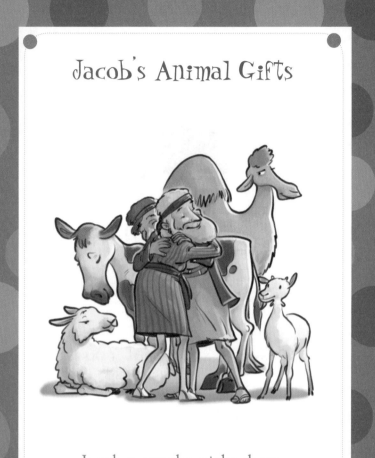

Jacob spent the night there.
He chose a gift for his brother
Esau from what he had with him.

Genesis 32:13 NIrV

Has anyone ever given you an animal for a gift? Was it because they loved you? Jacob gave someone animal gifts. Let's find out why.

One day God told Jacob to go back home to the country where he had been born. Jacob was afraid because he had stolen something important from his brother, Esau. He thought his brother would be angry with him.

Jacob obeyed God and started the long trip. He took his family and animals that God had given him.

Jacob sent some helpers ahead to tell Esau that he wanted to come home. The helpers came back and said, "We saw Esau. He is coming to meet you with four hundred men!"

Jacob was afraid. Four hundred men sounded like an army! So Jacob prayed for God to keep him and his family safe.

Jacob decided to send Esau a gift. Perhaps then Esau would forgive Jacob for stealing from him. So Jacob sent Esau many goats, sheep, camels, cows, and donkeys.

When Jacob saw Esau, he bowed down to show that he was sorry for the wrong thing he had done. Esau ran toward Jacob and hugged him. Jacob was forgiven—not because he gave many animals, but because Esau loved his brother.

Dear God, help me forgive those who do wrong things to me. Help me not to do wrong things to others. Help me to love everyone, no matter what. Amen.

Moses Takes Care of the Sheep

Moses was shepherding the flock of
Jethro, his father-in-law, the priest of
Midian. He led the flock to the west
end of the wilderness and came to
the mountain of God, Horeb.

Exodus 3:1 MSG

Sheep are cute but not very smart. They are helpless and need lots of protection. A group of sheep is called a *flock,* and the person who takes care of them is called a *shepherd.* Sheep were important to families in Bible times because they provided milk and meat, as well as wool to make tents and clothing.

Moses was the shepherd of his father-in-law's sheep. He led them to good water and delicious grass. Moses carried a big stick called a *staff* or *crook* to help guide and protect his flock.

One day while the shepherd Moses was out in the wilderness, he saw a burning bush. Moses was curious, so he came closer.

God spoke from the bush. "Moses! Moses!"

"Here I am," Moses said.

"Don't come any closer," God said. "Take off your sandals. The place you are standing is holy ground. I am your God."

When Moses heard this, he turned his face away. He was afraid to look at God.

"Go back to Egypt and help the people there," said God. "Bring them out of the land and to a land that I will give them."

Before Moses did what God asked, he made sure that his flock had a new shepherd. We have a good shepherd, too. His name is Jesus.

Dear God, thank You for Jesus, my Good Shepherd. Help me to follow Him always. Amen.

The Stick Becomes a Snake

Aaron threw his staff down in front of Pharaoh and his officials. It turned into a snake.

Exodus 7:10 NIrV

Snakes can be very tricky. Sometimes they blend in with the things around them, making them hard to see. This makes it easy for them to catch mice, birds, and frogs. Some snakes look like a stick. This story is about Aaron's stick (or shepherd's staff) that turned into a snake.

Moses was taking care of the sheep when God spoke to him. "Moses, go back to Egypt. The pharaoh is causing much trouble to My people. Ask Pharaoh to let the people go free."

God sent Moses and his brother, Aaron, to help the people get away from the bad pharaoh. When Pharaoh would not let the people go free, God told

Moses and Aaron what to do to show God's power. "Throw your staff down in front of Pharaoh. It will become a snake."

So they went back to Pharaoh. Aaron threw his stick down. It turned into a snake, just as God said it would.

Then Pharaoh called his magicians, and they turned their sticks into snakes, too. But Aaron's snake swallowed all the other snakes!

Snakes usually frighten people, but Pharaoh was not scared. He still would not let God's people leave Egypt.

Dear God, You are wiser
and more powerful than any
magician. Help me to be smart,
like You, not stubborn,
like Pharaoh. Amen.

Frogs Everywhere

So Aaron held his hand over
all the waters of Egypt, and the
frogs came up out of the water
and covered the land of Egypt.

Exodus 8:6 NCV

Did you know that a frog can jump twenty times its own length? That's pretty far! When Aaron stretched his stick over the water, frogs began to jump everywhere.

God sent Moses and his brother, Aaron, to ask Pharaoh to let the people of Israel go free. When Pharaoh would not let them go, God told Moses what to do.

"Tell Aaron to hold his stick over the rivers and ponds," said God. "The frogs will come onto the land."

Aaron did as Moses told him. Frogs came out of the rivers and ponds. There were big frogs and little frogs. The frogs covered the land. There were frogs in the houses. There were frogs in the beds and on the chairs. People sat on the frogs. They walked on the frogs. Frogs jumped on the tables. Frogs plopped in the food. The frogs jumped on Pharaoh and his people. But the frogs did not bother God's people.

The pharaoh called for Moses. "Take away the frogs," the king said. "I will let the people go." But Pharaoh did not keep his word.

God is not like Pharaoh. He *always* keeps His word. Now that's something to jump up and down about!

Thank You, God, for frogs.
And thank You for always
keeping Your word. It makes
me jump for joy! Amen.

Dust Becomes Lice

So the LORD said to Moses,
"Say to Aaron, 'Stretch out your rod,
and strike the dust of the land, so
that it may become lice throughout
all the land of Egypt.'"

Exodus 8:16 NKJV

Lice are ugly insects. They have hook-shaped claws and strong legs that hang on to hair. Lice crawl down the hair and make the skin itch. There must have been many itchy people and animals when God sent the lice to the people of Egypt!

For many years, God's people had been slaves to Pharaoh. God sent Moses and Aaron to Pharaoh many times but the Egyptian king would not let the people go free.

Once more Moses and Aaron asked Pharaoh to let the people go. And once again, Pharaoh said, "No!"

"Moses, tell Aaron to stretch out his staff," God said. "Tell him to strike the dust. It will turn to lice."

So Aaron did what Moses told him to do. When Aaron hit the dust with his stick, little bugs were everywhere. The lice hopped on the animals. They hopped on Pharaoh and his people.

Scratch, scratch, scratch went the people! *Scratch, scratch, scratch* went Pharaoh! *Scratch, scratch, scratch* went the animals! The lice made all the people and animals itch. But Pharaoh still would not let God's people go.

God can use any insect—even the ugly, tiny lice—to get people to obey Him.

God, You are Master of
everything—including me!
Help me to listen and then
do what You say. Amen.

A Swarm of Flies

"If you don't let them go, I will
send swarms of flies into your houses.
The flies will be on you, your officers,
and your people. The houses of Egypt
will be full of flies, and they will be
all over the ground, too."

Exodus 8:21 NCV

Flies are very icky insects. They have sticky pads on their feet, which helps them walk on the walls and ceiling. They also carry harmful germs. So the flies that God sent to the pharaoh and his people caused great problems.

God's people were slaves to Pharaoh. God wanted His people to go free so they could worship Him. He sent Moses and Aaron to talk to Pharaoh.

"Let God's people go with me so they can worship Him," said Moses to Pharaoh. "If you don't let the people go, God will send flies to cover the land."

But Pharaoh said, "No!"

So God sent a swarm of flies, just like He said He would do. The flies were everywhere. The ground was covered with flies. They were in Pharaoh's palace. In the houses, the flies walked on the walls and ceiling. They got into the food. People were swatting the flies, but the icky insects would not go away.

Even when the flies were everywhere and bringing disease to the people, Pharaoh still said, "No, I will not let the people go."

God can use any way and anything— even the pesky fly—to get someone's attention.

Dear God, You have my
attention. Show me how I
can be useful to You. Amen.

The Livestock Die

"If you refuse to let them go. . .
the LORD will bring a terrible plague
on your livestock in the field—
on your horses, donkeys and camels
and on your cattle, sheep and goats."
Exodus 9:2–3 NIV

The word *livestock* means the animals that live on the farm. They include cattle, horses, donkeys, goats, and sheep—even camels! Livestock was and still is important. Cattle, goats, and sheep give people meat, milk, and material for clothing. And horses, donkeys, and camels are used to carry things and people.

Moses and his brother, Aaron, had been to see Pharaoh several times. They had asked him to let God's people go free. But each time, Pharaoh would not let the people go with Moses. God had turned the river into blood. He had brought frogs to cover the land. He had caused the dust to change into lice. He had brought a large number of flies to destroy the land. But Pharaoh would not let the people go.

"If you do not let the people go this time," Moses told Pharaoh, "all the livestock—horses, donkeys, camels, cattle, sheep, and goats—will die."

Pharaoh said, "No!"

The next day, all the livestock of Pharaoh and his people died. Now the people would not have the good things that the livestock would have provided. But once again, Pharaoh would not let the people go.

God created each kind of livestock for a special job. Without each one of them, people would not have their daily needs met.

Thank You, God, for farm
animals and all the things
they provide. And thank You
for taking care of me every day.
Amen.

The Locusts Arrive

The LORD told Moses, "Raise your hand over the land of Egypt, and the locusts will come. They will spread all over the land of Egypt and will eat all the plants the hail did not destroy."

Exodus 10:12 NCV

A desert locust is a powerful jumper. Because of its strong legs, it can jump forty times the length of its body! Sometimes locusts come in big groups called *swarms*. Some swarms have as many as a billion locusts! That's a lot of locusts! They have sharp teeth and can eat a lot, just as they did in the land of Egypt.

Moses and his brother, Aaron, had been to Pharaoh many times. They had asked him to let God's people go free. Each time, Pharaoh said, "No!"

Once again God told Moses to talk to Pharaoh, and once again he said, "No, they cannot go free!"

God told Moses, "Raise your hand

over Egypt. Locusts will cover the land and eat everything that is growing in the fields."

So Moses did what God told him to do. Immediately, locusts covered the land.

Munch, munch, munch! They ate up everything that was growing in the fields. *Munch, munch!* They ate the fruit on the trees. Nothing green was left on the trees or plants.

Pharaoh called for Moses. "Take away the locusts," Pharaoh said. "I will let the people go." But Pharaoh did not keep his word.

Dear God, I don't want to be like Pharaoh. Please help me to keep my word to You and others. Amen.

Pharaoh's Horses and Chariots

The Egyptians chased them. All of Pharaoh's horses and chariots and horsemen followed them into the sea.

Exodus 14:23 NIrV

Horses are used for many things—riding for fun, police work, farm work, and more. In Bible times, horses were used to pull chariots.

God struck Egypt with ten plagues. Then Pharaoh finally said, "Yes!" when Moses asked him to let God's people go. Moses led God's people out of Egypt, where Pharaoh had kept them as slaves. They traveled day and night. God guided them by a pillar of cloud during the day and a pillar of fire at night.

After God's people left, Pharaoh changed his mind. He wanted them back. He told his men to go after God's people with horses and chariots.

When God's people stopped by the

sea, they saw Pharaoh's men coming behind them. They were scared. They had nowhere to run. The water was in front of them, and Pharaoh's men were behind them.

"Don't be afraid," said Moses. "God will take care of you." Moses raised his hands over the water.

Something amazing happened! God caused the wind to push the water back so the people could walk on dry ground. When all the people had crossed, the water flowed back together. Pharaoh's men, horses, and chariots tried to escape but were swallowed by the sea.

Pharaoh wanted to harm God's people, but our God kept them safe with His awesome power.

Dear God, You are more
powerful than anyone on earth.
Thank You for watching over
me all day and night, awake
and asleep! Amen.

God Sent Quail

That evening quail came and covered
the camp. In the morning the ground
around the camp was covered with dew.

Exodus 16:13 NIrV

Quail are short, stocky birds. Because their wings are short, they must beat them rapidly to fly. They spend much of their life on the ground, running and zigzagging through the grass. This made it easier for God's hungry people to gather the quail to eat when God provided this bird.

God's people were moving to a new home. They had brought food with them, but now the food was almost gone. There were no stores to buy more food.

The people began to grumble to Moses, their leader. "We are hungry," they said. "If we had stayed in Egypt, we would have plenty to eat. We will die without food. What shall we do?"

Moses talked to God. Then he told the people what God had said. "In the evening, you will see the glory of God. God isn't happy with all your grumbling, but He will take care of you."

That night God sent many quail to the people's camp. Now the people had plenty of meat to eat. They were happy because God took care of them. The people thanked God for His gift of food—the quail.

Dear God, help me not to be
grumpy and complain about
things. Remind me that You will
always give me whatever I need.
Thank You. Amen.

An Angel Leads the Hornets

"I will send hornets ahead of you.
They will drive the Hivites, Canaanites
and Hittites out of your way."

Exodus 23:28 NIrV

The hornet is an amazing insect. The queen hornet makes her nest of chewed up tree bark. She guards the nest of eggs, and stings anything that tries to harm her eggs. God used the hornets to drive out the enemies of the Israelite people.

Boom, boom, boom! the thunder sounded. The lightning zigzagged across the sky. A thick cloud covered the mountain. A trumpet gave a very loud blast. God was coming to visit Moses and the Israelite people.

God told Moses to come to the top of the mountain. He gave Moses the Ten Commandments and some other laws. He told Moses to explain the laws to the people.

So Moses came down from the mountain and began telling the people what God had told him. He told them about worshipping God on the first day of the week. He told them not to lie or steal and to get along with one another. He told them many other things.

Moses told how God's angel was going to lead them into a new land. God would send hornets to sting their enemies and run them out of the land—just like the queen hornet stings an enemy that tries to harm her eggs.

Thank You, God, for Your laws
that guide me. And thank You
for Your angels who do so many
amazing things. Amen.

Clean and Unclean Creatures

The LORD said to Moses and Aaron,
"Tell the Israelites this: 'These are the
land animals you may eat.'"

Leviticus 11:1–2 NCV

The Old Testament says it's okay if you eat grasshoppers! Gross!

Long ago, God gave Moses special instructions and laws which told God's people what creatures they could eat. The clean creatures could be eaten; the unclean creatures could not be eaten.

Land animals that chew the cud and have hooves that are separated completely in two are clean and can be eaten. Some of those kinds of animals are the oxen, sheep, goats, and deer.

Many creatures live in the water. Those that have fins and scales can be eaten. Most of the birds of the air are unclean and not to be eaten.

The insects that fly and also walk on

all four legs are not clean, unless they have joints in their legs and can hop. The insects that are clean to eat are the locusts, grasshoppers, katydids, and crickets. Yuck!

The laws in the Old Testament even told the people not to touch the unclean creatures. If an unclean creature falls on something, that item is not clean. That item must be put into water until evening, and then it will be clean.

The Israelites were God's people, and He wanted them to be pure and spotless when they worshipped Him. God made many laws that helped the people live happy, healthy lives.

Dear God, thank You for the food that I eat. Help me to eat things that are good for me, but maybe not grasshoppers! Amen.

The Two Goats

"Next Aaron will take the two goats and bring them before the LORD at the entrance to the Meeting Tent."

Leviticus 16:7 NCV

Goats are strong animals that can live almost anywhere. In Bible times, goats lived in the desert and were very important to a family. A goat provided milk and meat. The goat's hair made tents. The goat's hide made water bags.

In the Bible, male goats were used as sacrifices. Once a year, two male goats were brought to the Meeting Tent. God told the priest which goat would be offered to Him and which goat would be sent away. These two goats were used as offerings for the people's sins (the wrong things people did).

One goat was killed and burned on the altar. The priest would take some of the goat's blood and enter a special place called the Holy of Holies. The Holy of Holies was inside the Meeting Tent. This was a place God had set aside for the sacrifice. The priest asked God to receive the blood and offering to forgive the sins of the people.

Then the priest would send the live goat into the wilderness. This goat was called a *scapegoat*. The goat was left to wander about. This was to show the people that their sins were taken away.

Long before Jesus, God showed humans the meaning of forgiveness through the two goats.

Dear God, thank You for sending Jesus to die on the cross for my sins. Thank You for forgiving me when I do something wrong. You're wonderful! Amen.

The Snake on a Pole

The LORD said to Moses, "Make a
bronze snake, and put it on a pole.
When anyone who is bitten looks at it,
that person will live."

Numbers 21:8 NCV

There are many different kinds of poisonous snakes. Some live along the riverbanks, in the woods, in the deserts, or in the mountains. One day God sent poisonous snakes to the desert when His people were complaining.

Moses had led God's special people away from the bad pharaoh in Egypt where they had been slaves. Now they were angry with God and complaining to Moses.

"Why have you brought us to the desert to die?" they asked. "We have no bread or water. We hate the food God has given us."

So God sent poisonous snakes. They bit the people. Many of the people died.

The people came to Moses and said, "We did wrong when we grumbled to you and to God. We are sorry. Ask God to take away the snakes."

God told Moses to make a bronze snake and put it on a pole. "Anyone who is bitten by a snake can look on the bronze snake and live."

So Moses made a bronze snake and put it on a pole. When a snake bit someone, that person looked at the bronze snake and lived.

Today we don't need to look at a bronze snake. If we ever feel the bite of sin, all we have to do is look to Jesus. He'll save us!

Dear God, help me not to
grumble when I don't get what I
want. And thank You for Jesus.
He's the best Savior ever. Amen.

The Donkey Talks

The LORD made the donkey talk, and
she said to Balaam, "What have I done
to make you hit me three times?"

Numbers 22:28 NCV

Donkeys love to roll over on the ground. One day a man named Balaam had a donkey. She didn't roll over, but she did do some unusual things.

One day a king sent a message to Balaam. He would make Balaam rich if he would cause some bad things to happen to God's people.

Balaam saddled his donkey and traveled to see the bad king. God was angry with Balaam. So He sent an angel to block Balaam's way. The donkey left the road when she saw the angel. Balaam hit the donkey and got back on the road.

When the donkey saw the angel standing between two walls, she moved toward one wall. Balaam's foot was crushed. He hit the donkey again.

The third time the donkey saw the angel, she lay down. Balaam hit the donkey again.

God opened the donkey's mouth. "What have I done to make you hit me three times?" she said.

When Balaam started explaining why, God let him see the angel. The angel told Balaam if the donkey had not turned away every time she saw the angel, the angel would have killed Balaam but saved the donkey!

Animals have their own way of communicating with each other and us. But if God needed an animal to actually talk, it would. God can do all things.

Dear God, You are truly the
Master of me and all animals.
Help me to be gentle with every
living thing. Amen.

Samson Wrestles the Lion

They approached the vineyards of
Timnah. Suddenly a young lion came
roaring toward Samson.

Judges 14:5 NIrV

A lion is the strongest and most powerful of all the big cats. The lion needs much food to keep him strong. He kills and eats many animals. In Bible days, the lion was a danger to the shepherds who watched their flocks of sheep. Sometimes the lion would hide behind the rocks and bushes along the road, waiting to attack people. One day a lion was waiting to tackle Samson.

Samson was walking down the road with his father and mother. They were on their way to see a young woman Samson wanted as his wife. As they came close to a vineyard, a young lion came roaring out of the bushes.

Grrr-grrr-grrr! roared the lion as it

sprang onto Samson. *Grrr-grrr!*

Samson was probably surprised. The lion was strong, but God gave Samson much more power and strength. Samson tore the lion apart with his bare hands. It was so easy for him. God made him strong!

Lions are some of God's strongest creatures. But they're only as strong as God allows them to be. If God wants a man to win a fight with a lion, the lion doesn't have a chance!

God, You can make a strong
person even stronger! Help me to
remember that whatever strength
I have, I got it from You! Amen.

Honey from the Lion

Some time later, he [Samson] was going back to get married to her. But he turned off the road to look at the lion's dead body. Large numbers of bees and some honey were in it.

Judges 14:8 NIrV

Bees are like helicopters! Know why? Because God gave the bee special wings that allow it to fly in any direction—forward, backward, and sideways. A bee also does a little dance to show other bees where to find flowers with nectar. The bees then go bring the nectar back to the colony to be made into honey. Strong man Samson found an unusual place where bees had made honey.

Sometime earlier, a roaring lion had come at Samson. God gave him special powers to tear the lion apart with his bare hands.

Days later, as Samson was going down the same road, he thought about the lion he had killed. So he turned off the road to look at the lion's dead body.

Buzz-zzz! There as a large number of bees swarming around the body. Samson looked into the body and found that the bees had made honey in it. He reached in and dug out some honey with his hands. Mmmm, good. He shared the delicious honey with his mom and dad.

Each honeybee has a special job. The bees all work together to make honey that is not only delicious but good for you. That's bee-utiful!

Dear God, honey is good! Thank You for the bees that work together to make it. Help me work with others to make or do something good. Amen.

Foxes' Tails Tied Together

So Samson went out and caught
three hundred foxes. He took two
foxes at a time, tied their tails together,
and then tied a torch to the tails
of each pair of foxes.

Judges 15:4 NCV

Foxes are very speedy. Some run as fast as thirty-five to forty miles per hour! Because foxes can run fast, Samson thought of a way to use them against the Philistines—his enemies.

One day, Samson went to visit his wife. The wife's father, a Philistine, would not let him see her. So Samson got very angry with the father and all the Philistines.

"I am going to get even with them," said Samson.

Samson went out and caught three hundred foxes. He took two foxes at a time and tied their tails together. Then he tied a piece of wood on the tails of each pair of foxes. He lit the wood and turned the foxes loose in the fields of grain. The grain belonged to the Philistine farmers.

The foxes burned up all the grain that had been cut and stacked. They burned up all the grain that was still growing. They burned up the vineyards and olive trees. Samson turned the foxes loose because he was angry with the Philistines.

God gives us many things. Whether they are good or bad depends on how we use them. When we use things in anger, it hardly ever turns out good. Remember, the word *anger* is just one letter short of *danger*.

Dear God, help me to not get angry with others. Help me to love them and try to work things out. Amen.

The Sheep, Lion, and Bear

But David said to Saul, "I've been
taking care of my father's sheep.
Sometimes a lion or a bear would come
and carry off a sheep from the flock."

1 Samuel 17:34 NIrV

Lions can run up to fifty miles per hour! Bears are a little slower. They can run about thirty miles per hour. Both animals are a lot faster than we are! When a lion or a bear is hungry, it can attack another animal and make a fast getaway. So it was important for shepherds to keep a sharp eye on their sheep.

David watched his father's sheep. He would make sure the sheep had plenty of grass to eat and water to drink. He made sure no harm would come to them.

One day while David watched the sheep, a bear charged the flock. It grabbed a sheep and carried it away. David raced after the bear and struck it with his shepherd's staff. The bear rushed toward David, but he was not afraid. He knew God would protect him. He grabbed the bear by its hair, struck it, and killed it.

Another day, a lion sneaked up on the sheep. It grabbed a sheep and took off. David raced after the lion and took the sheep out of its mouth. The hungry lion dashed after David. With God's help, David grabbed the lion and killed it.

Bears and lions can be very fierce when hungry, but God protected David and his sheep, just like He protects us.

Dear God, thank You for helping us when we are in danger. With You by our side, we have the best protection ever. Amen.

Solomon Rides a Mule

He [David] said to them, "Take my officials with you. Put my son Solomon on my own mule. Take him down to the Gihon spring."

1 Kings 1:33 NIrV

A mule has two different parents. Its father is a donkey, and its mother is a horse. It has a short thick head, long ears, and short mane like a donkey. It is tall and has a shiny coat like a horse. Mules are used for riding and carrying very heavy things. King David rode on a mule and ordered his son Solomon to ride on a mule to be anointed as king.

Because King David was getting old, a new king was needed. King David had promised that his son Solomon would be the next king.

King David ordered the prophet Nathan, "Put my son Solomon on my mule, and take him to the Gihon spring," he said. "Have the priest anoint him as king over Israel. Then bring him back here."

So Nathan put Solomon on the mule and took him to the Gihon spring. The priest took an animal horn that was filled with oil. He anointed Solomon with the oil.

When the trumpet blew, the people shouted, "May King Solomon live for a long time!" The people were happy because they knew King Solomon would make good laws.

God created the mule to be sure-footed so it could carry baggage and people— even a king—through rough land.

Dear God, thank You for our leaders. Help them be sure-footed, make good decisions, and do good things. Amen.

Baboons and Apes

King Solomon also had many trading
ships at sea, along with Hiram's ships.
Every three years the ships returned,
bringing back gold, silver, ivory,
apes, and baboons.

1 Kings 10:22 NCV

Baboons and apes are very smart. They can remember lots of things and like to be with people. Many people keep them for pets. King Solomon had baboons and apes in his palace.

King Solomon was very rich. He had much gold. His throne was made of ivory and gold. His cups were made of gold. All the things used in the palace were made of gold.

King Solomon had many ships that would travel to different countries. His ships would bring gold, silver, and ivory to him. Sometimes the ships would bring unusual things such as baboons and apes.

The Bible does not tell what King Solomon did with the baboons and apes. Perhaps he just wanted something different than other kings.

King Solomon was richer than all the other kings on earth. Everyone who came to see King Solomon would bring a gift such as silver, gold, robes, weapons, spices, horses, and mules. King Solomon was very, very wise. He made good decisions for other people but not for himself. Even though Solomon had many things, he turned away from God.

Thank You, God, for the things
You have given me. Help me
share with others. Don't let the
things I have keep me away
from You. Amen.

Ravens Feed Elijah

"You will drink water from the brook.
I have ordered some ravens
to feed you there."
1 Kings 17:4 NIrV

Ravens are very wise and can solve many problems. Because these birds have a good memory, God used ravens to help Elijah. God knew they could take food to Elijah. The ravens showed Elijah how much God cared for him.

King Ahab was a bad king. He would not let the people worship God. God sent Elijah to talk to Ahab.

"I serve God, King Ahab," said Elijah, "but you do not obey Him. God told me the rain would stop."

With no rain, the land became dry, and the crops would not grow. God told Elijah that He would take care of him. He showed Elijah where to go.

"Stay and drink from the stream. I have told the ravens to bring you food," said God. Elijah obeyed God.

Caw, caw, caw! The ravens took care of Elijah. God had the birds bring Elijah bread and meat every morning. The birds brought bread and meat every evening. Elijah drank water from the stream.

Elijah obeyed God. He knew that God would take care of him.

Just like Elijah, God will take care of you. And He doesn't need ravens to do so!

Dear God, thank You for the food I eat and the water I drink. I know You will always take care of me. Amen.

The Bull on the Altar

"Get two bulls for us. Let Baal's prophets choose one for themselves, and let them cut it into pieces and put it on the wood but not set fire to it. I will prepare the other bull and put it on the wood but not set fire to it."

1 Kings 18:23 NIV

In Bible times, a bull was used as a sacrifice on the altar when people worshipped God. Elijah used a bull to help the people understand about God's power.

King Ahab had led the people to pray to a false god named Baal. Elijah asked the king's prophets to have a contest with him to see which god was the most powerful—the god Baal or Elijah's God.

"Put a bull on the altar," Elijah told the prophets. "Now pray to your god Baal and ask him to bring fire down to the sacrifice."

So the prophets prayed to their god. "Baal! Answer us!" they prayed but Baal did not answer.

Elijah laughed at the prophets. "Maybe Baal did not hear you," he said. "Call louder." So the prophets called louder, but their god did not hear them.

Then Elijah called the people to his altar. He placed a bull on it. "Pour water around the altar of stones, on the wood and bull," said Elijah. "Do this three times." Then he prayed to God. God heard his prayer and sent fire on the sacrifice. The stones, wood, and sacrifice burned down to ashes. Then the people worshipped Elijah's God.

God is all-powerful. He can do anything and everything.

Dear God, You are powerful
and can do mighty things. You
are my God. Help me to always
worship You and no other god.
Amen.

Elisha Plows with Oxen

Then Elisha left his oxen.
He ran after Elijah.

1 Kings 19:20 NIrV

Oxen are much stronger than horses. In Bible times, oxen were used for plowing the fields as well as pulling heavy loads. Most of the time, two or four pairs of oxen would do the work needed for each job. Oxen were very important animals.

God told Elijah that he needed a helper. As Elijah walked along, he saw Elisha plowing in his fields. Elisha was plowing with twelve pairs of oxen—that means twenty-four oxen. That's a lot of oxen!

Elijah went up to Elisha and threw his coat on him—which meant for Elisha to follow him. Elisha left his oxen and ran after Elijah.

"Let me go tell my father and mother good-bye," said Elisha. "Then I'll come with you."

"Go back," said Elijah.

Elisha went back, got two oxen, and killed them. He burned the plow to cook the meat of the oxen. He gave the meat to the people and they ate. Then Elisha started to follow Elijah. He became Elijah's helper.

Oxen are usually used in pairs. Two oxen joined by a yoke can double the work of one. After leaving his farmwork and oxen behind, Elisha was yoked with Elijah in a new job. Together they taught many people how to be prophets.

I want to follow You, Lord.
Show me what job You would
like me to do. Tell me who You
want me to work with. Amen.

The Bear Attack

Elisha turned around, looked at them, and put a curse on them in the name of the LORD. Then two mother bears came out of the woods and tore forty-two of the boys to pieces.

2 Kings 2:24 NCV

A bear can run very fast—much faster than a human. A bear has strong muscles so it can dig roots and bugs out of the ground to eat. The strong muscles help the bear to climb trees and tear apart its enemies. One day God sent two strong bears to help Elisha.

Elisha had just left Jericho. There he had done a miracle. Elisha made the water in the spring pure so the people could drink it again. Now he was walking down the road out of the city.

Suddenly some boys came out of the town and started making fun of Elisha.

"Go up, you baldhead!" they yelled again and again.

Elisha turned around and looked at

the boys. Then he put a curse on them in the name of the Lord.

Suddenly two mother bears came out of the woods. They attacked forty-two of the boys. They no longer bothered Elisha.

God does not like us to mock people who are different than we are. A good rule is this: If you can't say anything nice about someone, don't say anything at all. And if anyone makes fun of you, ask God to bless him or her. It may not change the mocker but it will make you feel better. And it will please God.

Dear God, help me to not make
fun of others. And if anyone
makes fun of me, help me forgive,
and then ignore them. Amen.

God Talks to Job about the Animals

"Job, do you give horses their strength?
Do you put flowing manes
on their necks?"
Job 39:19 NIrV

God created all the animals. And He did a good job, didn't He? He used many different colors to make many different animals. He gave some fur and some feathers. He made some big and tall. He made some small and short. Some are fat and some are skinny. Some have long tails and some have no tails. God must have had fun creating all the animals.

One day, God talked to Job about the animals. He asked Job who created the earth and everything that was in it. Then God began asking Job if he could make some of the things. God asked Job to think about who takes care of all the animals and gives them what they need.

Some of the things God asked were:

"Job, do you feed lion cubs?

"Do you know when mountain goat mommies have babies?

"Job, will the wild oxen agree to help you?

"Job, do you give horses their might?

"Do you order the eagles to fly way up high?"

Then God told Job that He was the Mighty One who takes care of all the animals. He was the one in charge of the world.

Thank You, God, for all the
different animals You have made .
Show me what I can do to help
take care of them! Amen.

Did Job See a Dinosaur?

"Look at the behemoth.
It is a huge animal.
I made both of you.
It eats grass like an ox."

Job 40:15 NIrV

The behemoth is a mystery creature. There is no animal on earth like it. In the Bible, the word *behemoth* may refer to today's hippopotamus. Some people think it means "dinosaur." The largest dinosaur was the Brachiosaurus. It was over eighty feet long and forty feet high. That's a BIG animal!

One day God was talking to Job about the different animals He created. He told Job about the behemoth that was strong and powerful. Its tail swayed back and forth like a cedar tree. Its bones were like bronze tubes and its legs strong like iron. The dinosaur was the largest land-living animal that ever roamed the earth.

God also described another mystery creature called the *leviathan*. It had a mouth with a ring of fierce teeth. Its back had rows of shields. Sparks of fire shot out of its mouth and smoke out of its nose. Perhaps this was a dinosaur called a Kronosaurus. Or perhaps a whale, a shark, or a crocodile.

Some animals living on the earth today have some of the traits of the behemoth and leviathan. But no animal has all the traits that God described.

We may not understand all of God's mysterious creations, but we do know that God is stronger than the most powerful animals. He is the mightiest of all!

Dear God, You are mightier than
any dinosaur that ever lived. So
I can sleep well, knowing You
are watching over me. Amen.

The Wise Ants

Go watch the ants, you lazy person.
Watch what they do and be wise.

Proverbs 6:6 NCV

A tiny ant is very strong! Depending on its species, an ant can lift and carry things that are three to twenty-five times its own weight! That is like you lifting three to twenty-five other kids your own size. That's strong! Ants live in colonies, much like a town. They depend on one another and help each other when they have a job to do. Working together, ants can find answers to hard problems.

In Bible times, wise men wrote many things that helped people make good choices. Solomon, a wise man, used the ant to show people how important it was to work together to get a job done well.

Solomon told lazy people to watch the ant. The ant goes out and looks for food. When it finds something, it lifts it and carries it back to its home. If something is too heavy for an ant to carry home, he calls other ants to come help. The ants store up food in their home so they will have something to eat when food is scarce.

We need to be wise like the ant—to work together to get things done. We also should always be prepared to help others—just like our friend, the ant.

Thank You, God, for the wise
ant. Make me strong. Help me
to work with other people to
get things done well. Amen.

Daniel and the Lions

"My God sent his angel. And his
angel shut the mouths of the lions.
They haven't hurt me at all."

Daniel 6:22 NIrV

The roar of a lion can be heard a long, long way off—five miles to be exact! But one day God shut the lions' mouths and they couldn't roar.

Daniel worked for a king named Darius. Daniel loved God and prayed to Him three times a day—morning, noon, and night.

Some men in the king's palace wanted to get rid of Daniel. So these royal officials tricked the king into making a new rule.

"Everyone must pray to me," the king told the people. "If you do not, you will be thrown into the lions' den."

The next day, the officials watched Daniel. Instead of praying to the king,

Daniel prayed to God. The men ran to the king. "Everyone must obey your new rule," they said. "Daniel was praying to God. He did not pray to you. Throw him into the lions' den."

The king was sad, but he had to obey the rule he had made. Daniel was thrown into the lions' den.

R-r-roar! The lions were hungry. But Daniel was not afraid. He knew God would take care of him. And God did just that! God sent an angel to shut the lions' mouths. The next day, Daniel was lifted out of the lions' den. Because he trusted in God, there was not a scratch on him.

Dear God, because I trust in
You, I am not afraid. You are
always good to me. Thanks for
watching over me! Amen.

Jonah and the Big Fish

The LORD caused a big fish to swallow
Jonah, and Jonah was inside the fish
three days and three nights.

Jonah 1:17 NCV

Fish come in many sizes, shapes, and colors. The biggest fish in the world today is the whale shark. This gentle giant is bigger than a school bus! One time God made a fish big enough to swallow a man. The man's name was Jonah.

God told Jonah to go to Nineveh and tell the people about God. Jonah did not want to go, so he got on a ship going the other way.

Who-oo-oo! The winds blew. The ship was tossed about. The sailors were afraid.

The ship captain yelled at Jonah, "Why are you asleep? Get up and pray for God to help us!"

Jonah told the men, "I'm the reason

for the storm. I ran away from God. Throw me into the sea and it will be calm."

The men threw Jonah into the sea. A big fish swallowed Jonah. *Gulp!* It was dark and smelly in the fish's belly.

"I am sorry for disobeying," prayed Jonah. "I will do what You want me to do, God."

Ugh! God caused the fish to throw up Jonah. Then Jonah went to Nineveh.

This story does not tell us what kind of big fish swallowed Jonah. But it does teach us that we can't run away from God. And it's always best to do what He wants us to do.

Dear God, let me know
what You want me to do.
Then help me do it. Amen.

Jonah and the Little Worm

Before sunrise the next day,
God sent a worm. It chewed the
vine so much that it dried up.

Jonah 4:7 NIrV

Worms are slimy insects. They have between one to five hearts! And if a worm is cut into two pieces, only the part of the body that has the head will live. One day a worm spelled trouble for Jonah.

After the big fish threw up Jonah, he obeyed God and traveled to Nineveh. There he told the people that God was going to destroy them because they were doing bad things. The people were afraid. They prayed to God with all their hearts. They said they would no longer do bad things. So God did not destroy them.

This made Jonah mad. He said to God, "I knew You might do something like this. That's why I didn't want to come in the first place!" Then Jonah sat down outside the city.

It was hot. So God made a vine grow beside Jonah to give him shade. This made Jonah very happy. Then before sunrise the next day, God made a worm to eat the vine. The worm ate so much that the vine dried up. Then God sent a hot wind and a burning sun. Jonah got mad again.

God told him, "You care more about this vine than you did about the people of Nineveh!"

Do you care more about other people than your own comfort?

Dear God, help me to love other
people more than I love the
things I have. Amen.

Shepherds Watch Their Sheep

That night, some shepherds were in the fields nearby watching their sheep.

Luke 2:8 NCV

A sheep's coat is called a *fleece*. It keeps the sheep warm in the winter. In the summer, sheep shed their coat to keep cool. In Bible times, shepherds took their sheep into fields to eat fresh grass. Sometimes they would spend the night in the fields. One night while poor shepherds watched their sheep, something unusual happened.

Baa, baa. The sheep snuggled close together as the shepherds watched over them. Suddenly the sky became bright. An angel appeared and the shepherds were afraid.

"Don't be afraid," said the angel. "I bring you news that will bring you joy. In the city, a Savior has been born. You will find the baby wrapped in strips of cloth and lying in a manger."

Suddenly many angels appeared in the sky. They praised God and said, "Glory to God way up in heaven. Let there be peace among the people on earth who please God."

When the angels disappeared, one of the shepherds said, "Let's go to Bethlehem and see these things."

The shepherds found Mary, Joseph, and baby Jesus, just like the angels had told them. They returned to their sheep, praising God.

God used sheep-watching shepherds as the first messengers of Jesus' birth. God picks the lowliest of men for the greatest of deeds.

Dear God, thank You for baby Jesus. Please use me to tell others the good news. Amen.

A Dove from Heaven

As soon as Jesus was baptized,
he came up out of the water. Then
heaven opened, and he saw God's Spirit
coming down on him like a dove.
Matthew 3:16 NCV

Unlike any other bird, a dove uses its bill to suck up water. It drops from the sky, skims over the water, and the bill reaches down to draw a drink. On the day Jesus was baptized, the dove that came down from heaven did not need a drink. That dove had more important things to do.

One day John the Baptist came out of the wilderness and preached to the people. He told them about Jesus who was coming. John told the people that they needed to be sorry for their sins and to be baptized.

While John was baptizing the people in the Jordan River, Jesus came walking toward him. "I want to be baptized," said Jesus.

"You have no need to be baptized," said John. "You have no sin."

"I want to set an example for others," said Jesus.

So John led Jesus into the Jordan River and baptized Him. When Jesus came out of the water, the heavens opened, sending the Holy Spirit down in the form of a dove.

A voice spoke. "This is My Son. I love Him. I am pleased," God said.

Doves are a symbol of peace and joy. Jesus, the Prince of Peace, gives us joy! Praise God!

God, You give me peace and joy!
Help me to be like Jesus and do
things pleasing to You. Amen.

A Net Full of Fish

When the fishermen did as Jesus
told them, they caught so many fish
that the nets began to break.

Luke 5:6 NCV

God has created fish to travel in groups called *schools*. When fish swim in such large numbers, they are safer from animals that want to eat them. It would seem easier to catch a school of fish than just one fish. But that wasn't happening to some men in a boat on the Sea of Galilee.

When people began to crowd around Jesus, he got into a boat on the Sea of Galilee. He told Simon Peter to move the boat out into the water. Then Jesus began to teach the people.

Later that day, Jesus said to Simon, "Go out into the deep water. Let down the nets so you can catch some fish."

"Jesus, we fished all last night and

caught nothing," answered Simon. "But we will do what You say."

Simon and the fishermen with him did what Jesus told them. They were surprised when they pulled up their nets full of fish. The nets were so full that they began to break.

"Come help us!" yelled Simon to the fishermen in a nearby boat.

The fishermen came and helped. They had so many fish they filled both boats! When we listen to Jesus, He blesses us beyond what we can imagine!

Dear God, thank You for all You have given me. Help me to share with others and to do what You tell me to do. Amen.

Jesus Teaches about the Moth

"Don't collect for yourselves treasures on earth, where moth and rust destroy and where thieves break in and steal."

Matthew 6:19 HCSB

Moths are strange creatures. They find their way at night by using the moon and the stars. Moths have hairy bodies so that they can stay warm when they fly. Some moths look much like their relative—the butterfly. Moths are very colorful and pretty, but some of the colorful moths are dangerous and even poisonous. Some moths like to eat holes in clothing and other things. Jesus used the moth to teach an important lesson.

One day Jesus sat on the mountainside and began to tell the people some important things about how they should live. The message He gave them is called "The Sermon on the Mount."

Jesus warned the people not to store

up treasures here on earth. Some of the treasures might be money, property, jewelry, and furniture. These things are good to have, but they are not the most important treasures. Moths and rust can destroy these things. Jesus warned the people that thieves might even steal their earthly treasures.

Jesus told the followers to store treasures in heaven instead, by doing good things for others and listening to God. Neither moths nor rust can destroy those treasures. What kind of treasures do you have stored up?

Thank You, God, for the earthly
treasures You have given me.
Help me store treasures in heaven
by doing good things for You
and others. Amen.

God Feeds the Birds

"Look at the birds in the air. They don't plant or harvest or store food in barns, but your heavenly Father feeds them. And you know that you are worth much more than the birds."

Matthew 6:26 NCV

There are over nine thousand kinds of birds in this world. Wow! That's a lot! How many birds can you name? There are cardinals, robins, sparrows, and bluebirds. There are blackbirds, woodpeckers, doves, and yellow finches. There are tiny hummingbirds and mighty soaring eagles. Some birds fly fast, and some birds do not fly at all. Some live in the South where it is warm. Some birds live in cold places. One day Jesus told a story about birds.

Jesus sat on a mountainside, teaching the people. He was telling them ways that would help them live better. Jesus told the people to be kind to others and to love their enemies. He told them to help others.

Sometimes it was difficult for people to understand what Jesus was saying. He tried to use words to paint them a picture. Jesus wanted the people to remember what He said.

Jesus told the people not to worry about what they would eat or drink or where they would live. He used the birds as an example. He said, "Look at the birds. They do not worry about eating or drinking. You are more important to Me than the birds. Trust Me to take care of you."

The next time you feed a bird, remember how God takes care of you.

Dear God, I trust You to take care of me. Please show me how I can help to take care of others—even birds. Amen.

Fish for Lunch

"Here is a boy with five loaves of barley
bread and two little fish, but that is
not enough for so many people."

John 6:9 NCV

About thirty thousand different kinds of fish share this planet with us! The Bible does not name the kinds of fish that were caught in the seas and lakes of Israel. But it does tell us that one day Jesus used only five barley loaves and two fish to feed a hungry crowd.

Jesus and His helpers sat down on the mountainside. Soon more than five thousand people had gathered around. They wanted to listen to Jesus tell them about God.

Soon evening came and the people were hungry. Jesus told His helpers, "Give the people something to eat."

One of the helpers said, "We don't have any food."

Just then, Andrew came to Jesus with a little boy. "This little boy wants to share his lunch. But he only has five small bread loaves and two fish. That's not enough to feed so many people."

Jesus said, "Tell the people to sit down on the grass."

Jesus took the bread and fish and thanked God for the food. Then He broke the food into pieces. Jesus gave the food to the people and everyone had enough. Later the helpers gathered up twelve basketfuls of leftovers!

When you are not sure what to do, give Jesus what you have. He'll do the rest!

Dear God, You are amazing!
Show me how to use what You
have given me. Amen.

The Wolf and the Sheep

"A hired man is not a real shepherd
. . . . He sees a wolf come and runs for
it, leaving the sheep to be ravaged
and scattered by the wolf."
John 10:12–13 MSG

Wolves are great jumpers. A full-grown wolf can jump as high as ten feet! Wolves can smell things up to almost two miles away! A wolf looks much like a dog, but it isn't friendly like a dog. It is a fierce and dangerous hunter that usually feeds on small animals. But sometimes it will attack and kill deer, sheep, and even cattle. Jesus used the wolf in a story to teach people He would always protect them.

Jesus said He was the Good Shepherd and the people were His sheep. Like people, sheep can be scared easily. They need a shepherd they can trust to lead, protect, and take care of them.

Jesus said He would give His life for

His sheep. But a man hired to take care of the sheep would not. Because he didn't own the sheep, the hired man would leave the sheep at any sign of danger. When he saw a wolf coming, the hired man would run away and leave the sheep to be eaten.

Jesus used the example of the sheep and wolves to show us that we don't need to be afraid. As long as we are in Jesus' care, nothing can really harm us. He is our wonderful Good Shepherd!

Dear God, thank You for being
such a Good Shepherd. I know
I don't have to worry about
anything because You're
watching over me. Amen.

Pigs Run into the Sea

A large herd of pigs was
feeding there on the hillside.
Luke 8:32 NIrV

A full-grown pig weighs as much as six hundred to eight hundred pounds. That's as heavy as a piano! A pig likes to wallow in wet mud to keep cool. One day Jesus came across a legion of demons and a herd of pigs.

Jesus was passing through an area when a man controlled by demons met Him. The man had not worn clothes in a long time. He lived in a graveyard instead of in a house. The man was so wild that people were afraid of him. They tried to bind him with chains but he was so strong, he broke them.

When the man saw Jesus, he told Him his name was Legion because he had so many demons inside of him.

Not very far away from the man was a herd of pigs. The demons inside the man begged Jesus, "If you make us leave this man, send us into the herd of pigs."

Jesus said, "Go!"

The demons came out of the man and went into the pigs. The pigs ran down the steep cliff into the lake and drowned. Then the man was free of demons. He was so happy he asked Jesus if he could go with Him. But Jesus said, "Go home, and tell others what I have done for you."

Dear God, Your Son, Jesus,
did some pretty amazing things.
Give me the right words to tell
others about Him. Amen.

The Son and the Pigs

"The son wanted to fill his stomach
with the food the pigs were eating."
Luke 15:16 NIrV

Pigs will eat almost anything—including worms, dead insects, tree bark, and garbage—yuck! Pigs are *omnivores*, which means they eat both plants and meat. One day a young man wanted to eat pig food!

A man had two sons. The younger son said to his father, "Give me part of your money. I don't want to wait until you die to get it."

The younger son took his money and traveled to a faraway land. He spent all his money having a good time. Soon he had no money left, not even for food to eat.

The son got a job feeding pigs. He was so hungry he wanted to eat the pigs' food.

Then he thought about his father. "Why am I here?" he said. "At home even the servants have plenty to eat. I will go home and tell my father I did wrong. I will ask for a job."

The father saw his son coming and ran to hug him.

"Father, I have done wrong," said the son.

The father called to his servants, "Quick! Bring my son the best robe, a ring for his finger, and shoes for his feet. Let's celebrate! My son has come home."

Like the son's father, God will always welcome us back, no matter what we've done!

Dear God, thank You for
forgiving me. Tonight I will
sleep well, knowing You will
always welcome me with
open arms. Amen.

The Good Samaritan and His Donkey

"Then he put the hurt man on his own donkey and took him to an inn where he cared for him."

Luke 10:34 NCV

Donkeys are funny and helpful. They wiggle their floppy ears to keep cool. A donkey needs to cool off after carrying people and pulling heavy wagons. Jesus told a story where a donkey did something special for someone.

One day a man was walking down the road when some robbers grabbed him. They beat him and took his money. They left the bleeding man lying there.

Along came a priest from the temple. Did he stop and help the man? No! He walked by on the other side of the road.

Next came a Levite, a helper to temple priests. When he saw the hurt man, he walked over and looked at him. But did he help the man? No! He, too, left the man lying there.

Then along came a Samaritan man on a donkey. The hurt man was a stranger to him, but he stopped to help him. He put medicine on the man's cuts and bruises. Then he put bandages on him.

Did the Samaritan man leave the hurt man beside the road? No! He put him on his donkey and took the injured man to an inn where he could heal.

Jesus wants us to help others, just like the kind Samaritan man and his faithful donkey helped the hurt man. Are you a good Samaritan?

Thank You, God, for this story.
I want to help others, too.
Please show me a way I can be
a good Samaritan. Amen.

Worth More than Sparrows

"Aren't five sparrows sold for
two pennies? Yet not one of them
is forgotten in God's sight."
Luke 12:6 HCSB

A sparrow is a tiny, noisy bird that has lots of energy. It likes to build nests in unwanted places—gutters, pipes, and chimneys. In Israel, boys still sell sparrows in the marketplace. After they catch a sparrow, they tie a string to one of its legs. Then they tie four or six of them together. These birds then fly around over the boys' heads.

Sparrows are of little value and sell for a very small amount of money. Jesus used sparrows to show how much God loves His creatures.

One day Jesus was telling people that they need not be afraid of any one man or woman, boy or girl. Because God's people are precious to Him, they don't need to be afraid of what anyone says or does to them. The only one that people should hold in awe is God.

Then Jesus used the sparrows as an example to show the people about God's love. Jesus said, "God does not forget even one of the sparrows. God even knows the number of hairs on your head! So don't be afraid. You are worth more than many sparrows."

If God cares even for the smallest birds, how much more does He care for you?

God, I'm so glad that You created all the animals—big ones and small ones. Thank You for caring so much more for me than even the sparrows. Amen.

Money from a Fish

"Go to the lake and throw out your fishing line. Take the first fish you catch. Open its mouth. There you will find the exact coin you need."

Matthew 17:27 NIrV

$Fish$ have strong muscles along their sides to help them swim. Those muscles help the fish to swim in an "S" pattern, to wiggle from side to side. The swishing of the tail also helps the fish to move forward in the water. When the fish wiggles, it is harder to catch. Several of Jesus' disciples—Simon Peter, Andrew, James, and John—were fishermen. They left their boats to follow Jesus. But Peter went back to his old job whenever Jesus told him to.

Some men were always trying to get Jesus in trouble. One day, the tax collectors came up to Peter. "Does Jesus pay the temple tax?" they asked.

Peter said, "Yes, He does."

When Peter walked to the house where Jesus was staying, he told Jesus about the tax collectors.

"We don't want to make the tax collectors angry," said Jesus. "So go to the lake and throw out your line. Take the first fish you catch. Open its mouth and you will find a coin. Give it to the tax collectors for our taxes."

Peter did just that and it really paid off!

Even creatures in the deep sea are commanded by Jesus. When we all work at obeying Him, we are always rewarded!

Dear God, I want to do the work You want me to do. Show me how I can serve You tomorrow. And the next day, and the next! Amen.

The Sheep and the Shepherd

"The one who enters through the gate
is the shepherd of the sheep."

John 10:2 NIrV

Sheep can hear very well, but they do not like loud noises. The shepherds in Bible times spoke quietly to the sheep. The shepherds named each of the sheep, and the sheep would respond to their shepherd's voice. Jesus told the people a story about a good shepherd.

Jesus' talked about a shepherd who entered the door of the sheepfold. (A *sheepfold* was a pen or shelter where the sheep were kept.)

"The shepherd calls the sheep and they know his voice," said Jesus. "He is the only one the sheep will follow. If anyone else comes into the sheepfold and tries to call the sheep, they will not follow him. They will run away because he is a stranger."

The people did not understand what Jesus was trying to tell them. So Jesus explained the story.

"I am the shepherd," said Jesus. "I am the only way through the door to the sheepfold. Follow Me."

Jesus continued talking to the people. "Some other people may tell you to follow them, but they are like thieves and robbers. Do not listen to them. They will not lead you in the right way. I am the Good Shepherd. You must follow Me."

Your shepherd Jesus knows your name. Do you hear Him calling?

Dear God, I love my Good
Shepherd. Jesus knows my name,
and my heart knows His voice.
I will go wherever He calls me.
Amen.

The Lost Sheep

"He calls his friends and neighbors
together and says, 'Rejoice with me;
I have found my lost sheep.'"

Luke 15:6 NIV

Sheep stay close together for protection. But if frightened, they will run in all directions. Sometimes a sheep will get lost. Jesus told a story about a lost sheep.

A shepherd had a hundred sheep. Every morning he would take his sheep to the hillsides. *Baa, baa,* went the sheep as they followed him. The sheep drank the cool water, ate the green grass, and rested in the shade. The shepherd loved his sheep and protected them.

When night came, the shepherd took his sheep to a pen called a *sheepfold*. The pen had no door so the shepherd slept across the doorway. "Nothing will hurt my sheep," he said.

Each night before he went to sleep,

the shepherd counted his sheep. One night he began counting. "There's one, two, three, four, five. . . ." He counted all the way to "Ninety-eight, ninety-nine. . ."

Suddenly the man stopped counting. One sheep was missing. "Lost sheep!" called the man. "Come to me!" The shepherd looked everywhere for his lost sheep.

Then he heard a quiet little sound. *Baa, baa.*

There caught in a thorn bush was the lost sheep! The happy shepherd picked him up and carried him home on his shoulders.

Jesus is like that shepherd. If you ever stray, He will find you and bring you home!

Dear God, I am so glad that You
are here to take care of me.
I will never get lost if I stay
close to You! Amen.

Jesus Rides on a Donkey

They brought the donkey and the colt
to Jesus and laid their coats on them,
and Jesus sat on them.

Matthew 21:7 NCV

Donkeys are very strong. In Bible times, they were a symbol of peace and royalty.

Donkeys are used for carrying people and things and sometimes for working in the fields. Most of the time, Jesus walked with His disciples, but one day He rode on a donkey.

Jesus called His disciples to Him. "Go into the next village, and you will find a donkey with a colt. Untie both of them and bring them here to Me. Tell the owner that Jesus needs them."

The disciples went into the village and did as Jesus asked. When they brought the donkey and colt to Jesus, the disciples spread their coats on them.

Then Jesus rode on the donkey.

As the disciples and Jesus came close to Jerusalem, crowds of people began spreading their coats on the road. Other people cut branches from the trees and placed them on the road.

All the people shouted, "Hosanna to the Son of David! Blessed is He that comes in the name of the Lord! Hosanna in the highest!"

Because Jesus rode into Jerusalem on the donkey the people understood He was a man of peace—and the King of kings!

Jesus is my King, God!
He is my Lord. Praise Jesus!
The Prince of Peace! Amen.

Jesus Drives the Animals from the Temple

He [Jesus] also turned over the benches
of those who were selling doves.

Matthew 21:12 NIrV

Have you ever been to a farm or zoo when the animals were making lots of noise? What would happen if it was that noisy at church? One day Jesus found the temple, the place where people worshipped God, very noisy.

When Jesus went into the temple, He saw people were everywhere. People were shouting at each other. Some people were selling animals and other people were buying animals. It was very noisy. It did not seem like a place of worship. It sounded like a busy street or a playground at recess.

Moo-moo! went the cows. *Baa-baa!* went the sheep. *Coo-coo!* went the doves. When Jesus heard all the noise and saw all the people and animals and money, He was unhappy.

In the temple, everyone was supposed to be quiet and walk softly. It was a place for people to pray, sing praises, and hear stories about God. It was not supposed to be a place of business.

So Jesus tipped over the tables of money and chased out the people selling animals. Jesus stood in the middle of the temple and quoted a Bible verse: "My house shall be called the house of prayer."

Once Jesus cleared out the temple, He healed people who were blind and disabled. Jesus brought peace.

Dear God, help me to not yell
and run when I am at church.
May it be a place where I can
sing and pray and hear the
stories about Jesus. Amen.

The Hen Gathers
Her Chicks

"I have wanted to be like a hen who
gathers her chicks under her wings.
But you would not let me!"
Matthew 23:37 NIrV

A mother chicken, called a *hen*, is pretty amazing. She can hear her baby chick in its shell when it is almost ready to hatch. When the hen hears the chick go *peep-peep*, she will gently *cluck* to the chick. She is telling her little one it is time to break out of the shell. The hen is very protective of her chicks, even when they are still in the eggshell. She keeps them under her wings where they can stay warm and out of danger.

When Jesus taught people, He often used different animals in His stories, to help people understand. In one lesson He used the example of a hen and her chick.

One day Jesus was teaching some

important truths to a crowd of people. He told them they were to love God with all their heart. Then they were to love one another. But some people didn't want to listen. They wanted Jesus to go away.

Jesus told the people He felt sorry for them. He had wanted to gather the people even as the hen gathers her chicks under her wing for protection, safety, warmth, and comfort. But many of the people would not let Jesus protect them.

Jesus wants to protect you today and forever. Will you let Him?

Jesus, I want You to gather me
under Your wings where I can be
safe and warm. Thank You for
loving and wanting me so much.
Amen.

The Rooster Crows

The Lord turned and looked straight at Peter. And Peter remembered what the Lord had said: "Before the rooster crows this day, you will say three times that you don't know me."

Luke 22:61 NCV

Male chickens called *roosters* are early-morning crowers. On top of this crower's head is a large red growth called a *comb*. The flap of red skin hanging under his beak is called a *wattle*. One day the rooster's crowing—*cock-a-doodle-doo*—reminded Peter of what Jesus had said earlier.

After a meal with His disciples, Jesus told them He would be leaving and they would not be able to follow. Peter said, "I will lay down my life for You."

Jesus said, "Before the rooster crows, you will say you do not know Me three times."

Later when the soldiers arrested Jesus, Peter followed Him to the courtyard. A servant girl asked him, "Are you one of the disciples?"

Peter said, "No, I am not."

As Peter warmed himself by the fire, he was asked, "Are you one of the disciples?" Again Peter said, "No, I am not."

Then someone who had been with the soldiers who arrested Jesus asked Peter, "Didn't I see you with Jesus?"

Just as Peter said, "No," a rooster began to crow. *Cock-a-doodle-doo!* Peter, reminded of what Jesus had said, was sorry for what he did.

Later Jesus forgave Peter. He allowed Peter to make a fresh start.

The rooster's crow—*cock-a-doodle-doo*—reminds people it is time to arise. They, too, have a fresh start on a new day.

Sometimes I need to start
things over, Lord. Thank
You for always giving me
a second chance. Amen.

The Great Catch of Fish

Jesus came and took the bread and gave
it to them, along with the fish.

John 21:13 NCV

Fish can be hard to catch sometimes. They are slippery and like to hide among their surroundings. Fishing was an important business on the Sea of Galilee. Many fishermen owned boats and would go searching for schools of fish. They would catch them, bring the fish into town, and sell them.

After Jesus died on the cross, His followers were very sad. Peter, one of Jesus' disciples, said, "I'm going fishing."

"We will go with you," said the other disciples.

They went out on the sea in the boat and fished all night. They caught nothing. Just as the new day began, they saw someone on the beach. The person called, "Have you caught anything?"

They answered, "No!"

"Throw the net on the right side of the boat. You will find fish," the person said.

John recognized the person and said, "It is Jesus."

When Peter heard this, he leaped into the water and swam to meet Jesus. The other disciples rowed to shore, dragging their net full of fish. When they got to the land, Peter helped drag in 153 fish!

Jesus said, "Come and eat." Then He took the bread and fish and gave it to the disciples.

When we use what we have and obey Jesus, we find we have more than enough!

Here I am, Lord. I am ready to listen to You. I know that when I obey You, You will make sure I have more than enough. Amen.

The Queen's Official, a Horse, and a Chariot

On his way home he [the queen's official] was sitting in his chariot. He was reading the book of Isaiah the prophet.

Acts 8:28 NIrV

A horse has a built-in flyswatter! His tail swishes back and forth to keep the flies away. In Bible times, people used horses to pull their chariots.

One day a queen's official had ridden his chariot to Jerusalem to worship. On the way home, he stopped in the desert to read from the Bible.

Suddenly a man named Philip, one of Jesus' followers, came up to the official's chariot. "Do you understand what you are reading?" asked Philip.

"No. I need someone to tell me what it means," said the man. "Will you help me to understand it?"

So Philip got into the chariot and they rode off together. Philip and the man read the Bible scroll. "Who is this man I am reading about?" said the official.

Philip told the man about Jesus. "God sent Jesus to the earth. Jesus is God's Son! Jesus loves you."

The man was happy to hear this good news. As they were riding down the road, they came to some water. The man said, "Look! Here is some water! I want to be baptized."

So Philip baptized the man. The official was glad Philip had told him about Jesus.

We can help people learn about Jesus, too—anytime, anywhere!

Dear God, thank You for people
who help me understand the
Bible. Give me the words to tell
someone else about Jesus. Amen.

The Snake Bites Paul

Paul shook the snake off into the fire.
He was not harmed.

Acts 28:5 NIrV

POISONOUS snakes can be dangerous. They have long, hollow fangs that fold back against the roof of their mouth. When a snake strikes, it unfolds its fangs, which shoot forward, stabbing its prey. Paul, a follower of Jesus, met up with a poisonous snake when he was shipwrecked on the island of Malta.

Whoo-oo, whoo-oo! The wind blew. *Splash, splash!* The waves rose high. *Pitter-patter! Pitter-patter!* The rain fell. The ship was tossed around in the sea.

"Men, don't be afraid," said Paul, who was traveling on the ship. "An angel told me that we would be safe."

Before the ship could reach land, it hit rocks and broke into pieces. All the

276 men on the ship made it safely to the island.

It was cold and rainy. The island people built a fire to keep the men from the ship warm. Paul picked up some sticks and threw them on the fire. A poisonous snake came out of the sticks and sank its fangs into Paul's hand. Paul shook the snake off into the fire.

The people thought Paul would die from the snakebite. Paul was not afraid. He told the people God would keep him safe from harm. And that's just what God did!

Later, Paul healed many sick people on the island. God was with him!

Dear God, help me to remember
to always trust in You. With
You on my side, I know I
can be brave. Amen.

The Future Animal Kingdom

Then wolves will live in peace
with lambs, and leopards will
lie down to rest with goats.

Isaiah 11:6 NCV

Some day when Jesus Christ, the Prince of Peace, returns, all animals and all people will live together in harmony! There will no longer be *predator* (an animal that hunts for food) or *prey* (the animal hunted and eaten). How cool is that?

Instead of chasing, attacking, and eating lambs, wolves will be a friend to the sheep. Leopards will lie down and sleep with goats. Little calves and young bulls will eat with lions instead of being eaten *by* lions. And a little child—perhaps you—will lead lions, leopards, and all other animals wherever he or she wants! That's how tame all the ferocious animals will be!

Even mommy cows and daddy bears will eat together while their calves and cubs sleep side by side in the grass. Like oxen, lions will eat hay. And a cobra will be so gentle and kind that a boy or girl could play beside the snake's hole. A child will even be able to put its hand in a poisonous snake's nest, and the viper will not hurt the child.

What a wonderful world that will be! Until that day comes, we must be careful around dangerous animals. But it's great to know that the peace Jesus gives us now is the same peace that will one day rule the world!

Dear God, I am excited about
Your future kingdom, when I
can sit and pet lions and bears.
What a day that will be! Amen.

JANE LANDRETH enjoys touching young lives with God's love. She has taught children in school and church settings. Jane enjoys watching and learning about animals, an activity she shared with her son when he was young, and now shares with her two grandsons.

Jane and her husband, Jack, live in the Ozarks, where she continues writing for children. They enjoy watching the different animals around their yard and in the fields and forest nearby.

This is Jane's fourth book for Barbour Publishing—her third *Bedtime* book.

Other Bible Bedtime Titles
from Barbour Publishing

Bible Devotions for Bedtime
978-1-59310-358-3

Bible Prayers for Bedtime
978-1-60260-066-9

Bible Blessings for Bedtime
978-1-60260-975-4

Bible Miracles for Bedtime
978-1-60260-692-0

Available wherever books are sold.